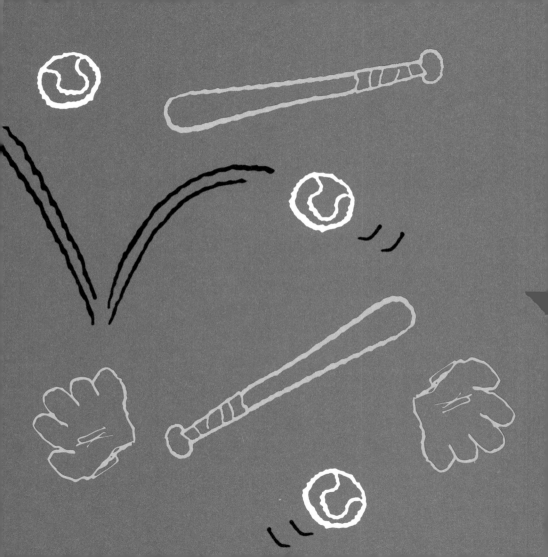

Insights From The Outfield

by

Schulz

CollinsPublishers

A Division of HarperCollins*Publishers*

The
Dream Team

..AND EVERYONE WHO MADE THE TEAM THIS YEAR GETS A NEW CAP!

HERE YOU GO, SCHROEDER.. YOU DESERVE IT..

THIS IS FOR YOU, SNOOPY, OL' PAL!

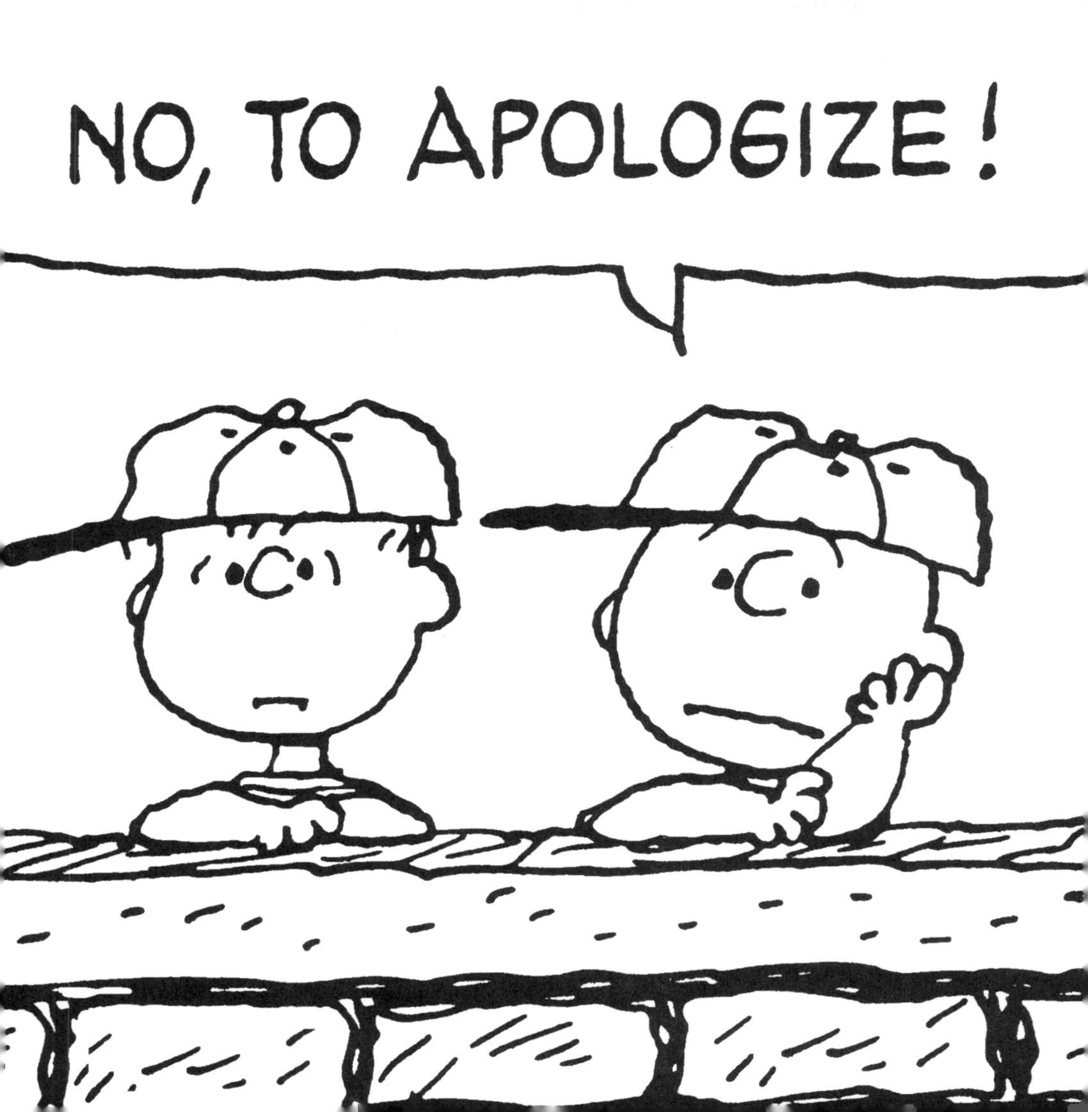
NO, TO APOLOGIZE!

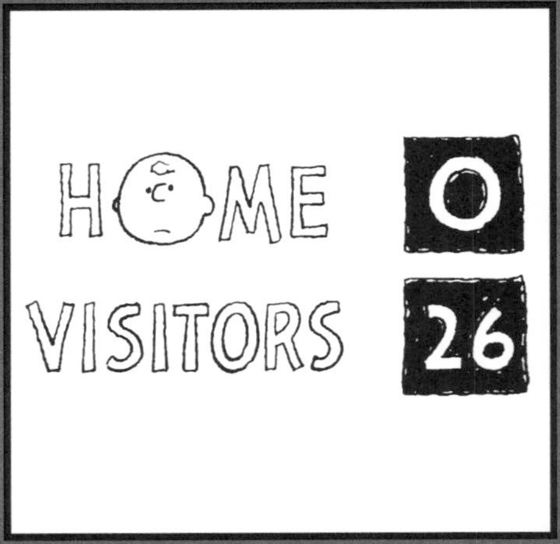
HOME 0
VISITORS 26

It's How
You Play The
Game

 It's How You Play The Game

Memoirs
From The
Mound

Memoirs From The Mound

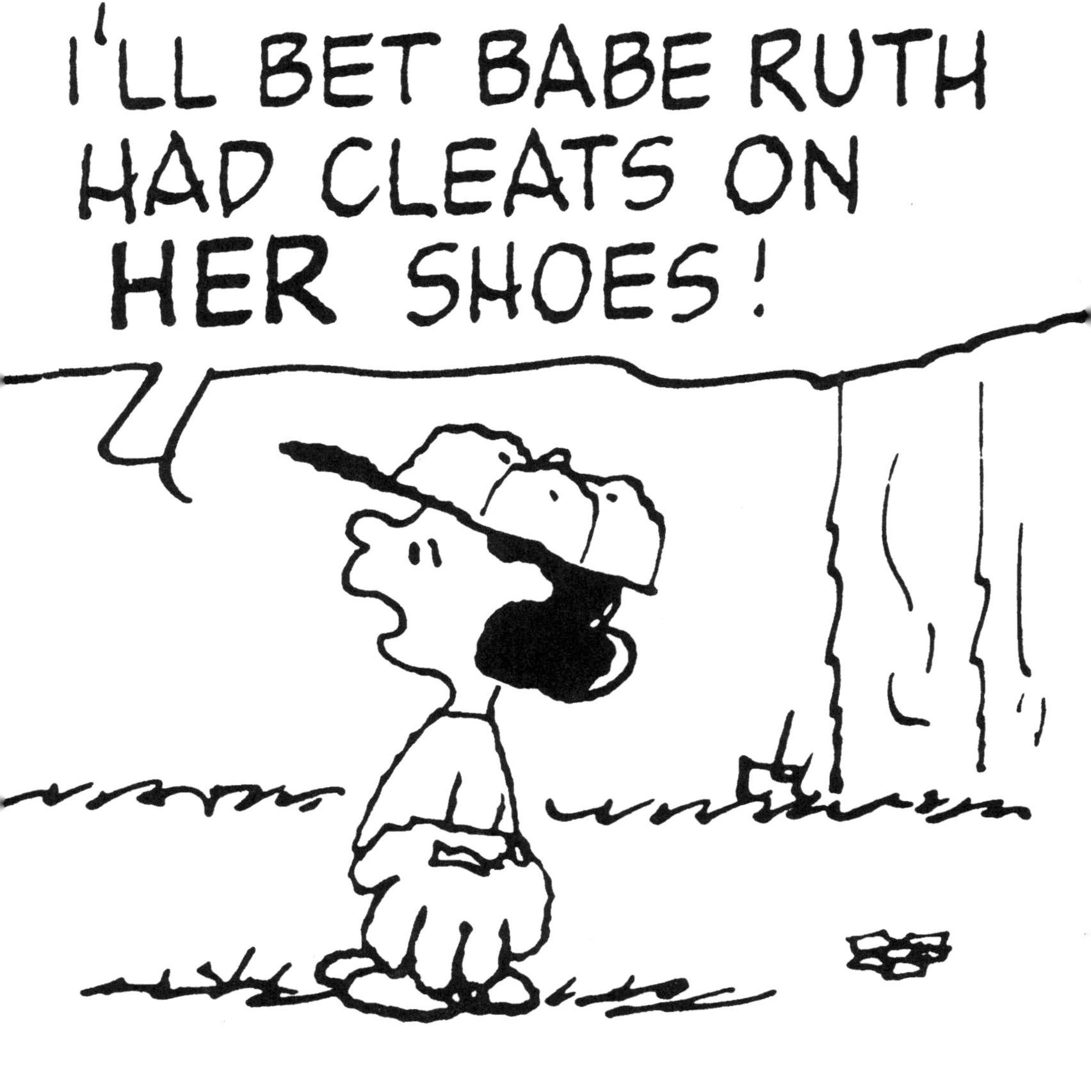
I'LL BET BABE RUTH HAD CLEATS ON HER SHOES!

Memoirs From The Mound

A Packaged Goods Incorporated Book
First published 1997 by CollinsPublishers
10 East 53rd Street, New York, NY 10022
http://www.harpercollins.com
Conceived and produced by Packaged Goods Incorporated
276 Fifth Avenue, New York, NY 10001
A Quarto Company

ISBN 0-00-649234-7

Printed in Hong Kong

1 3 5 7 9 10 8 6 4 2

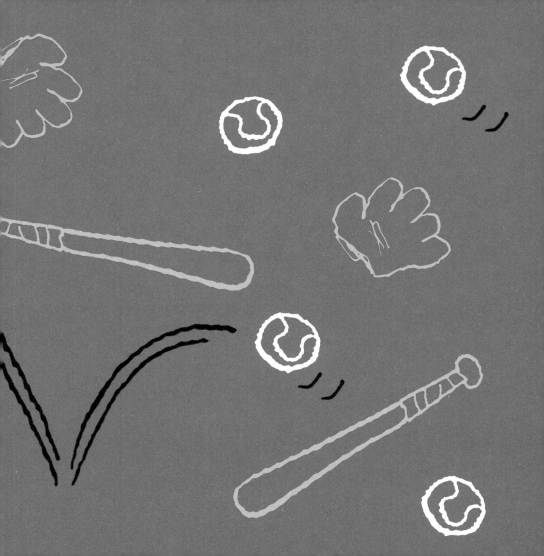

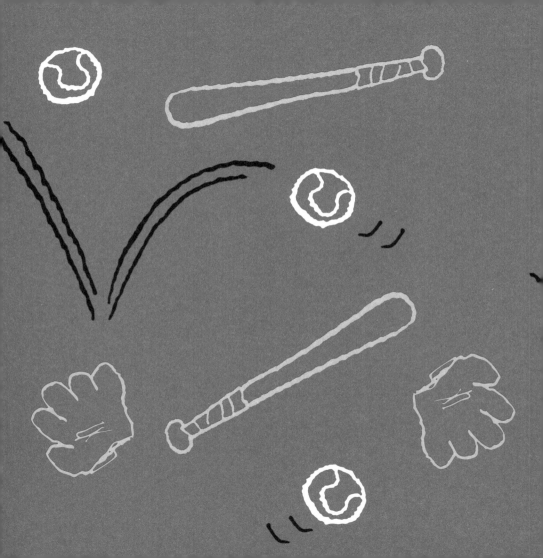